D0407582

GAME-CHANGING ATHLETES

BILLIE JEAN KING

The Battle of the Sexes and Title IX

Kate Shoup

Cavendish
Square

New York

Published in 2016 by Cavendish Square Publishing, LLC
243 5th Avenue, Suite 136, New York, NY 10016

Copyright © 2016 by Cavendish Square Publishing, LLC

First Edition

Library of Congress Cataloging-in-Publication Data

Shoup, Kate, 1972-
Billie Jean King: the Battle of the Sexes and Title IX / Kate Shoup.
pages cm. — (Game-changing athletes)
Includes bibliographical references and index.
ISBN 978-1-5026-1053-9 (hardcover) ISBN 978-1-5026-1054-6 (ebook)
1. King, Billie Jean. 2. Tennis players—United States—Biography. 3. Women tennis players—United States—Biography. 4. Tennis—Tournaments—History—20th century. 5. Sex discrimination in sports—United States. I. Title.
GV994.K56S56 2016
796.342092—dc23
[B]
2015028947

Editorial Director: David McNamara
Editor: Fletcher Doyle
Copy Editor: Rebecca Rohan
Art Director: Jeffrey Talbot
Designer: Joseph Macri
Senior Production Manager: Jennifer Ryder-Talbot
Production Editor: Renni Johnson
Photo Research: J8 Media

CONTENTS

When Billie Jean (Moffitt) King was born in 1943 to working-class parents, no one could have imagined she would grow up to be a champion in the country-club sport of tennis, but that's exactly what happened. The girl who learned to play on the public courts of Long Beach, California, went on to win 183 **singles** titles, 39 **Grand Slam** titles (in singles, **doubles**, and **mixed doubles**), and two "**Wimbledon triples**" (winning singles, doubles, and mixed doubles in the same year). But Billie Jean wasn't just a champion on the tennis court. Indeed, it was what Billie Jean achieved *off* the court that made her truly exceptional.

Exhibit A: Thanks in part to Billie Jean's outspoken nature, the tennis establishment changed its rules to allow professional players to compete in its more prestigious tournaments, including the four Grand Slams: the Australian Open, the French Open, Wimbledon, and the US Open. This allowed athletes like Billie Jean to earn a living by playing the sport they loved.

Exhibit B: It was Billie Jean who led the charge for equal pay for male and female players. Early on, women on the pro tennis circuit often earned just one-eighth of what men did. Billie Jean risked her career to change that. Today, all four **Grand Slam tournaments** (and many others) offer equal pay for male and female players. For

Billie Jean, it wasn't just about the money, however. The purpose of her efforts was "to enable women to play and to make people pay attention."

Of course, Billie had her critics—those who felt that female athletes weren't on par with the men and therefore didn't deserve equal pay. However, Billie Jean silenced them when, in 1973, she defeated Bobby Riggs in the "Battle of the Sexes." Billie Jean's triumph was a victory not just for female athletes but for all women. As noted by the *New York Times*, "In a single tennis **match**, Billie Jean King was able to do more for the cause of women than most feminists can achieve in a lifetime."

Later in life, Billie Jean would take on yet another cause: LGBT rights. After being outed by a female lover in 1981, Billie Jean began what she called "the most difficult struggle I've had in my whole life": her struggle with her sexuality. Today, Billie gladly supports such LBGT-oriented organizations as the Gay Games, the Gay and Lesbian Alliance Against Defamation (GLAAD), and the Elton John AIDS Foundation.

Not surprisingly, Billie Jean has received countless awards and honors in recognition of her tireless efforts on behalf of diversity—including an Arthur Ashe Courage Award and a Presidential Medal of Freedom. (Billie Jean was the first female athlete ever to win the latter award.) But for Billie Jean, life was never about winning awards. It was about caring and being her best. "The main thing is to care," she said. "Care very hard, even if it is only a game you are playing."

President Barack Obama gave Billie Jean King the honor of being the first female athlete to receive the Presidential Medal of Honor on August 12, 2009.

Billie Jean Moffitt, shown before her twentieth birthday, was determined to be the best at something from a young age.

CHAPTER 1

OPPORTUNITIES LACKING

"I had a great sense of destiny from
the time I was very young."

—Billie Jean King

On November 22, 1943, twenty-one-year-old Betty Moffitt welcomed her first baby, a girl, to the world. Betty, who was born in Taft, California, but had since moved to the seaside town of Long Beach, had wanted to name her newborn Michelle Louise. Instead, Betty—like so many new mothers during the tumultuous years of World War II—decided to name the baby after the baby's father, Bill Moffitt, a US Navy man who had been stationed across the country in Virginia. The baby was christened Billie Jean Moffitt. Billie Jean, or "Sissy" as the family called her, "was a little angel," said her mother.

When Billie Jean's father was released from active duty at the end of the war, he returned to Long Beach to live with Betty and Billie Jean. He found work as a firefighter while Betty stayed home to care for Billie Jean. In 1948, the couple had another child, Randall James—Randy or R.J. for short.

Bill and Betty bought a small home in Long Beach. "We lived in a neat tract house in a nice neighborhood,"

Billie Jean recalled. "We had three bedrooms for my parents, Randy, and me; the bad news is that we only had one bathroom." She noted, "I did have my own bedroom, even if that's about all it was—room for a bed."

Life with the Moffitts

The Moffitts were like many families of their time. "Dad made the money and Mom ran the home," said Billie Jean. But, she added, "The two of them shared a lot of the work around the house." She continued, "I grew up with a good sense of teamwork between a man and a woman."

Billie Jean's father was, in the words of Joanne Lannin, author of *Billie Jean King: Tennis Trailblazer*, a "tall, square-jawed man with blue eyes and wavy brown hair." Billie Jean described him as "a jock." He played baseball and ran track, but his favorite sport was basketball. He was such a capable player that the NBA offered him a tryout, but he declined. "I had already been born," explained Billie Jean. "To my father, being a family man meant providing security, so he opted for a job with a regular paycheck and good benefits."

Billie Jean's mother enjoyed being active—she was an excellent swimmer—but was less interested in sports than her husband. "My mother was a pretty traditional 1950s homemaker," said Billie Jean. Betty was, however, "big on perseverance and seeing things through." This led Billie Jean to sometimes call her mother the "velvet hammer."

Both Billie Jean and R.J. played sports from a young age. Billie Jean played softball and R.J. played baseball.

Billie Jean's father carved a bat for Billie Jean with his own hands. Billie Jean loved to play and became an excellent hitter. "Whenever the fire department had a picnic," her father said, "the men would always want Billie Jean to play shortstop or third base." He continued, "She had a natural ability in hitting the ball and fielding and throwing." R.J. would go on to play twelve years as a Major League pitcher, mostly for the San Francisco Giants. However, Billie Jean quickly realized "there was no place for an American girl to go in the national pastime."

The truth was, when Billie Jean was a child, there were few opportunities for girls and women to play *any* sport. Many people believed that girls and women lacked the physical stamina to participate in athletic endeavors. Others thought participation in sports would damage their health. The International Olympic Committee even barred women from participating in more vigorous events. For example, women were not permitted to participate in track and field events until 1928. Even then, they were not allowed to run farther than 800 meters (0.5 miles). Because so many women collapsed at the end of the 800-meter event, it too was banned until 1960. Needless to say, longer-distance events were also off the table. It was not until 1972 that a 1,500-meter (0.9 mi) race was added to the list of women's events. Incredibly, the first Olympic women's marathon would not be run until 1984.

Still, sports or no, Billie Jean always believed she would be a success. Once, when she was only five or six years

Billie Jean King: The Battle of the Sexes and Title IX

Female athletes compete in the 80-meter hurdles during the 1952 Olympics. This was one of only a few events in which women were eligible to compete.

old, she proclaimed to her mother that she would be the best at *something*. (Billie Jean's mother "just smiled and kept peeling potatoes or doing whatever she was doing," said Billie Jean.) Billie Jean and her brother used to sit at the dining-room table and practice signing autographs. "I put a great deal of thought into how I would make my *M's*," said Billie Jean. She dreamed of being more than just Billie Jean Moffitt of Long Beach, CA. When she was a little girl, Billie Jean used to stand in front of the world map in her classroom and "stare at all the places that I wanted to visit."

Billie Jean's Introduction to Tennis

During the 1950s, when Billie Jean was a girl, tennis was, as Billie Jean described it, "a country-club sport"—although interestingly, it was considered adequately ladylike for girls to play. The Moffitts, however, "definitely were not a country-club family." And so, said Billie Jean, "Tennis was not on our radar."

That changed when Billie Jean was eleven years old. One day, Susan Williams, a friend from school, invited Billie Jean to play tennis at the Virginia Country Club in Long Beach—*the* place for the elite of Long Beach. Situated on a 135-acre (54.6-hectare) tract of land, the Virginia Country Club featured a golf course, clubhouse, and, of course, tennis courts, where Susan and Billie Jean played. "I didn't know what I was doing," said Billie Jean, "but we had a great time hitting (with me whiffing a few, probably) balls over the court."

Although she had fun with Susan, Billie Jean didn't give tennis much thought after that first outing. "I knew that if I could only play tennis at the country club, there was little chance of me playing it on a regular basis." That changed a few weeks later when Billie Jean's softball coach told her about a nice gentleman who offered free tennis lessons at Houghton Park in Long Beach each Tuesday. "That was all I needed to hear," said Billie Jean.

The "nice gentleman" who offered free tennis lessons was Clyde Walker. He'd spent most of his career teaching tennis at country clubs but had recently taken a job in the Long Beach Recreation Department. "He felt that he would never find anyone at a club with the grit to become a champion," said Billie Jean. The public parks, he believed, might be a better spawning ground.

After just one tennis lesson with Clyde, Billie Jean was hooked. "In the span of a couple of hours, Clyde made tennis come alive," she said. "He made it *fun*." When her mother picked her up from that first lesson, Billie Jean informed her of her new life's ambition: to be the number one tennis player in the world. She had found her *something*.

A New Passion

Billie Jean knew that if she wanted to be the best tennis player in the world, she had to practice more than once a week. Fortunately, she quickly ascertained that Clyde Walker gave tennis lessons at other Long Beach parks throughout the week. "He was amazed to find me at another park, miles away, and a third park the day after that, and so on," she said.

Billie Jean was missing just one thing: her own tennis **racket**. Her parents told her if she wanted one, she would have to buy it herself—but Billie Jean was just eleven years old. She was too young for a job. Where would she get the money? "I decided I would go to some of our neighbors looking for work," she said. She took out their trash, tidied their gardens—"anything they asked me to do," she recalled.

Unable to wait any longer, she took all the money she had saved up—a whopping $8.29—to Brown's Sporting Goods. There was just one racket in her price range: it had purple strings and a purple grip. Billie Jean was thrilled— purple was her favorite color! She loved the racket so much she slept with it every night.

Tennis uses a unique scoring system. To win a match, a player must win a prescribed number of **sets**, usually two out of three. To win a set, a player must win a minimum of six **games**. However, the player must win by at least two games. In other words, if Player A wins six games and Player B has won five, play must continue. If Player A wins the next game, he or she wins the set. If Player B wins the next game, then the players are tied, and they now play a tiebreaker. (The tiebreaker was invented by Jimmy Van Alen, and it was used at the US Open for the first time in 1970.) In a tiebreaker, the first person to win seven points wins the set—but he or she must win by at least two points.

A BRIEF HISTORY OF TENNIS

According to historians, tennis—from the French word *tenez*, which means "to hold," "to receive," or "to take"—was first played in the twelfth century in northern France. At first, players used the palm of their hand to strike the ball. Later, they used a glove. By the sixteenth century, the glove had been replaced by a racket, from the Arabic word *rakhat*, or "palm of the hand." In those days, tennis was played indoors. This form of the game was called "real tennis."

European royalty adored real tennis. In England, Henry V (1387–1422) was among the first to play. His descendant Henry VIII (1491–1547) was passionate about the game. Francis I of France (1494–1547) was known to play, as was his successor, Henri II (1519–1559).

During the eighteenth and early nineteenth centuries, real tennis died out. In its place came lawn tennis. This form of the game was played outdoors on an hourglass-shaped grass court. Slowly, the game's popularity grew. In 1874, the first lawn tennis court was built in the United States, at the Staten Island Cricket and Baseball Club.

Modern tennis is much like lawn tennis, except the shape and dimensions of the court are different. The court is no longer shaped like an hourglass but is a rectangle. In addition, the net is lower in the modern game, and the court surface may vary. Some courts are grass, some are asphalt, some are synthetic, and some are clay. Finally, modern tennis may be played indoors or outside.

Jack Kramer coaches an all-male group from the country-club set in 1954. Kramer was a great player but later opposed equal tournament purses for female players.

In June 1955, just nine months after her first lesson, Billie Jean played in her first tournament: the Southern California Junior Championships. She handily beat her first opponent, but she lost her second match, two sets to one. Billie Jean was discouraged, but she kept at it. By 1958, at the age of fourteen, she had become a force on the junior circuit in Southern California, ranked second in the fifteen-and-under division.

Billie Jean: Outsider

Billie Jean may have taken to tennis, but at first, tennis—or at least the tennis establishment in Southern California— did not take to her. As noted by Susan Ware, author of *Game, Set, Match: Billie Jean King and the Revolution in Women's Sports*, "In the 1950s and early 1960s, tennis really wasn't all that changed from the **genteel**, country-club sport it had been in the 1920s and 1930s." Billie Jean, who came from a working-class family, simply did not fit in.

Billie Jean felt particularly persecuted by Perry T. Jones. Known as "Mr. Tennis of the West Coast," Jones ran several tournaments in Southern California. Once, Jones—whom Billie Jean later described as "a fussy old bachelor who hated girls"—refused to allow Billie Jean to sit for a group photo of players at the Southern California Junior Championships because she was wearing shorts and a blouse (which her mother had sewn for her) rather than a traditional tennis dress. ("Don't worry, Mom," Billie Jean told her humiliated mother. "He'll be sorry someday.")

While the other tennis families could easily absorb the costs associated with playing the game—equipment, coaching, travel to tournaments, and so on—the Moffitts struggled to make ends meet. After all, they didn't just support Billie Jean in her efforts on the tennis court, they also supported R.J., who was becoming ever more capable on the baseball diamond. "My dad was often working two jobs and my mom sold Tupperware and Avon in order to be able to afford my and my brother's activities," Billie Jean said in the book *Billie Jean*, written with Frank Deford. She added, "I look back now and am still amazed at how much they sacrificed for my brother and me."

Nonetheless, Billie Jean said, "We weren't nearly as poor as it was fashionable to make us out to be." She added, "It was just that anybody in tennis who wasn't in the country club was always stereotyped as indigent." Billie Jean noted, "I certainly never felt deprived in any way, although especially as I got into tennis and encountered people who lived with so much more, I understood better how many things there were that we could not manage." If anything, she viewed this disparity as a benefit. "Being a little bit disadvantaged in a middle-class world gave me a great drive," she said.

For their part, Bill and Betty made these sacrifices willingly, and they didn't get too bogged down on their kids' results. "They didn't ask me if I won or what the score was," Billie Jean remembered. "All they cared about was my happiness and whether or not I had done my best."

While Billie Jean developed on the tennis court, younger brother Randy Moffitt excelled on the baseball diamond. He spent twelve years in the major leagues as a relief pitcher.

It wasn't just her family's finances that cast Billie Jean as an outsider. The fact that she was a girl also worked against her. Although girls were encouraged to play tennis, they inevitably got less attention from coaches and other members of the tennis establishment than boys did. "The boys invariably got all the breaks," Billie Jean said. She recalled watching coaches at the L.A. Tennis Club falling all over themselves to help a mediocre male player improve his **serve**. "I wanted to scream out, 'Just give me five minutes, five lousy minutes!'" she said. "But of course, nobody bothered."

Physical Challenges

When it came to tennis, Billie Jean's working-class upbringing and gender certainly worked against her, but these were nothing compared to her physical challenges. For one thing, Billie Jean had terrible eyesight: 20/400. According to the American Optometric Association, this is considered "severe visual impairment." When Billie Jean started wearing glasses at the age of thirteen, it was, she said, "incredible. I could see the ball—imagine!" But only a very few players wore glasses. In fact, many people told Billie Jean that she'd never become a champion due to her eyesight. Not surprisingly, "that only got my back up and made me all the more determined," said Billie Jean.

Billie Jean also suffered from breathing problems. "I inherited sinus trouble from my mother and chest problems from my father," she said. As a result, she often experienced difficulty in breathing during play. Incredibly, despite her high level of play, Billie Jean also struggled with her weight. "Even as quick and as fast as I've been," she said, "I've been fat all over at times, with chubby little legs." An article in the *New York Times Magazine* in 1967 listed her generously at five foot six inches tall (1.67 meters) and 140 pounds (63.5 kilograms). Other sources listed her at five foot four inches (1.63 m). "That is when everything is going right," she told the magazine. "I love to eat." Still, Billie Jean played on. She had a dream, and she intended to make it come true.

The incomparable Alice Marble, who won eighteen Grand Slam titles between 1936 and 1940, provided valuable coaching to a young Billie Jean Moffitt.

CHAPTER 2

BILLIE JEAN BREAKS OUT

"You'll never make it, so don't bother."

—Tennis great Maureen Connolly to Billie Jean King

I n 1959, Billie Jean played in her first major tournament, the US Championships. (The US Championships, now called the US Open, is one of four Grand Slam tournaments each year. The others are the Australian Open, the French Open, and Wimbledon.) She was fifteen years old. Billie Jean lost in the first round to sixteen-year-old Justina Bricka of France, but the experience wasn't all bad. Billie Jean won the first set 6–4 and very nearly won the second one—and the match—as well, but Bricka stormed back for the win.

That same year, Billie Jean met Alice Marble, who had won eighteen Grand Slam titles from 1936 to 1940. Marble, who in addition to being a notable player had also served as a spy for the United States during World War II, saw real talent in Billie Jean and began coaching her during the weekends.

Training with Marble made a big impact on Billie Jean. She rose in the US rankings from number nineteen to number four. Perhaps more importantly, said Billie Jean in an interview with the *Long Beach Press-Telegram*, "For the first time in my life, I sensed some kind of legacy that I was a part of." Marble was impressed with Billie Jean. "Clyde Walker has given Billie all the tools she needs to be a winner," Marble said. "Now all she needs is confidence and time."

Young Billie Jean had plenty of time. Confidence was another matter. She wrote in *Billie Jean* that her confidence was greatly shaken by another great player, Maureen Connolly. Connolly, who was the first woman to win all four Grand Slam tournaments in the same calendar year (1953), a feat that is itself called a Grand Slam, told Billie Jean, "You'll never make it, so don't bother."

The next year, 1960, brought marked progress. Billie Jean won her first tournament title—the Philadelphia and District Women's Grass Court Championships—but she continued to struggle, particularly against veteran players. Dorothy "Dodo" Cheney, at age forty-three, defeated young Billie Jean at the Southern California Championships and again at the US Hard Court Championships; thirty-five-year-old Dorothy Head Knode bested her at the US Women's Clay Court Championships; and Margaret Osborne duPont, at forty-two, beat Billie Jean at the Pennsylvania Lawn Tennis Championships. Billie Jean still had a lot to learn.

Billie Jean's International Debut

In 1961, Billie Jean defended her title at the Philadelphia and District Women's Grass Court Championships and won the Pennsylvania Lawn Tennis Championships. That same year, Long Beach resident Harold Guiver, who would later work as a sports agent before becoming an executive with the Los Angeles Rams football team, helped raise money to send Billie Jean to England for the famous Wimbledon tournament. Billie Jean skipped her high school graduation at Long Beach Polytechnic High School to fly to London.

In her first Wimbledon, she lost in the second round of the singles draw. However, Billie Jean and fellow American Karen Hantze claimed the doubles title—the youngest and the first **unseeded** duo ever to do so. Billie Jean was just seventeen years old.

Billie Jean's doubles victory at Wimbledon was especially sweet because her beloved coach, Clyde Walker, was dying of cancer. Billie Jean remembered, "He'd often told me of his own dream to coach a player through a Wimbledon win. It was very important to him, and so very important to me." She continued, "He held on and died the day after Karen and I won 6–3, 6–4. I was so happy to give him that last bit of gratification."

Despite her success, some saw Billie Jean as an unlikely champion. Sportswriter Frank Deford described her as a "chubby little thing with the hideous, tacky glasses"; *Time* magazine called her "the chunky, bespectacled little Californian"; and *Sports Illustrated* noted that Billie Jean "stands 5 feet 6 inches tall, has brown hair, light blue eyes, a small impertinent nose and a weight problem." Like so

Billie Jean (*far left*) was seventeen years old when she and Karen Hantze beat Margaret Court and Jan Lehane O'Neill (*near right*) in the Wimbledon doubles final in 1961.

many women, Billie Jean was judged for her appearance rather than her achievement. Another man, a so-called "supporter" of Billie Jean, had a different interpretation: "You'll be good because you're ugly, Billie Jean." No doubt, these barbs bothered Billie Jean, but she didn't let them stop her. Whatever hurt or anger Billie Jean felt, she channeled it into her tennis game.

Steady Improvement

In the years that followed, Billie Jean continued to improve her game—although it was not always smooth sailing. She failed to win a single tournament in 1962. She did, however, manage a major upset at Wimbledon, defeating the world number one and top-seeded player Margaret Smith in the second round. (Billie Jean reached the **quarterfinals** of that tournament but lost to Ann Haydon-Jones.)

In 1963, Billie Jean claimed her first international singles title at the Irish Open. She also won the Southern California Championships. At Wimbledon, she advanced to the final. Her opponent was again the great Margaret Smith. This time, Smith emerged victorious. Smith felt, according to a story in the *New York Times*, that this was due to Billie Jean's lack of practice. "You've got all the shots," Smith told Billie Jean, "but I always wear you out." She continued, "You just don't play enough."

Why didn't Billie Jean play enough? Because she was also a student at Los Angeles State University. This cut into her time for tennis. Worse, Billie Jean had to take a job to cover her schooling. Despite being a nationally ranked player, Billie Jean did not qualify for an athletic scholarship simply because she was a woman. This was especially galling because many male players, with whom she frequently practiced and often defeated on the court, went to school for free.

In 1964, heeding Smith's advice, Billie Jean decided to leave school to play tennis full time. "I still had my dream of being number one in tennis, but I had yet to win a major singles title," she said in *Billie Jean*. "I finally realized that I would never know whether I could make it unless I made a commitment to play full time." Bob Mitchell, a businessman from Melbourne, offered to pay Billie Jean's way to his home country, Australia, to train. "I told my friends I was going to Australia to become the best player in the world," said Billie Jean.

In Australia, Billie Jean worked for three months with coach Mervyn Rose to improve her game. As noted by journalist Hal Higdon, "The Australians had her running, doing exercises and participating in two-on-one drills." At first, Billie Jean could barely last five minutes with these drills. "The first three or four weeks, I thought I was going to die," Billie Jean told the *New York Times*. When her time in Australia was up, however, "she could retrieve shots for an entire hour," said Higdon. "Mervyn Rose had a huge impact on me," Billie Jean said. He did more than just improve her fitness, however. "Taking lessons and playing with him totally changed my game and put the finishing touches on my playing style."

At first, changing her game did not produce the results Billie Jean was looking for. "Although I was ranked in the top five in the world, I was having trouble beating run-of-the-mill Aussie players in minor state championships," recalled Billie Jean. She lost in the **semifinals** at the Australian Championships (now called the Australian Open) and again at Wimbledon. At the US Championships, Billie Jean made it to the **finals** to play Margaret Smith—who had since married and changed her name to Margaret Court—but lost. The loss was, according to Billie Jean, "devastating." However, she noted, the match itself proved to her that she was "good enough to be the best in the world." She went on to declare, "I'm going to win Wimbledon next year!"

Love and Marriage

In the fall of 1962, while a student at Los Angeles State University, Billie Jean met a young man named Larry King (not to be confused with the talk-show host of the same name). Like Billie Jean, he was an avid tennis player. He played on the school's team. (Ironically, Larry, who was a mediocre player at best, had a full athletic scholarship.) By the following spring, the two were a couple and in October of 1965, after Billie Jean's time in Australia, they were married. Billie Jean Moffitt became Billie Jean King. Her husband would have a profound effect on her career and on her developing views of feminism.

By then, Billie Jean had committed to tennis full time. That meant she was away much of the time. Larry had his own pursuits. He was busy finishing his undergraduate degree, after which he attended law school. "It's probably better we're apart so often," Billie Jean told *Sports Illustrated* in 1968. "When we are together we just enjoy each other so much, not much law gets read and I don't get much practice in."

Larry was incredibly supportive of Billie Jean's career. This was unusual at a time when most men expected their wives to stay home and tend to the house and, eventually, children. Incredibly, Billie Jean considered quitting tennis and becoming a housewife, but Larry set her straight. "Billie Jean," he said, "I just don't see how you can give up something where you have the potential to be the best in the world—the best of all." Sometimes, fans asked for his autograph. Often, he signed it "Mr. Billie Jean King."

He seemed to identify with the women's movement even before Billie Jean did. It was Larry who pointed out how unfair it was that he, a "second-rate player," had received a tennis scholarship to Los Angeles State University while Billie Jean, a "far superior competitor," did not.

Larry, who attended law school during the early days of Billie Jean's professional career, went on to work as an attorney and real estate developer. He also functioned as a tennis promoter, noting that, "I've probably promoted more women's tennis tournaments than anyone in the world." Often, he worked side by side with Billie Jean in her various endeavors both on and off the court. The two worked well together. "As it happens," he has said,

Billie Jean Moffitt and Larry King were married on September 17, 1965.

"Billie Jean's forte is identifying the problem and mine is identifying the solution."

The Prime Years

By the end of 1966, Billie Jean had achieved her goal. She was the number one player in the world. But it was an honor she would have to share with Maria Bueno, a Brazilian. That year, Billie Jean's high ranking was due in no small part to her success at Wimbledon, where she claimed the singles title—her first of many Grand Slam singles crowns.

In 1967 and 1968, Billie Jean stood alone at the top of the heap. In 1967, she won the singles, doubles, and mixed doubles titles at both Wimbledon and the US Championships. The next year, she emerged victorious at the Australian Championships and again won the singles title at Wimbledon—her third in a row. She was, in the words of *Sports Illustrated*, "an established star."

Billie Jean had learned an important lesson from Margaret Court: practice and training are paramount. Each day, when not on tour, Billie Jean was on the court by 10 a.m. for two hours of drills. At noon, she broke for lunch. After that, Billie Jean challenged one of the local men to a match, followed by three or four sets of doubles with her chief doubles partner, Rosie Casals. Finally, at six or seven in the evening, Billie Jean would pack it in to cook dinner for herself and her husband, Larry.

On the court, Billie Jean was fiery and animated. "You idiot!" she'd shout when she made a mistake. Or, "Move your feet!" Or, if she was really upset, "Peanut butter and jelly!"

The press took note. As written in the *New York Times*, "The bespectacled tomboy from Southern California is the liveliest personality to hit the international circuit in years. She has courage and she has color, a combination rarely found in tennis today." The fans loved her. Billie Jean was a star.

Perhaps more gratifying, Billie Jean's fellow players—male and female—respected her. Male superstar Arthur Ashe said of Billie Jean, "She's a hell of an athlete." Billie Jean even won over Maureen Connolly—the player who, in 1959, had told Billie Jean she would never make it. "Billie Jean just has to rate as the ultimate," Connolly told *Sports Illustrated*. "What she has is that rare ability to rise to the necessary pressure threshold and stay there for the big ones—those moments when it's 30-all and you've missed the first serve and you have to get the second one in. Billie can get it in." Connolly added, "Billie's a great champion."

The Advent of the Open Era

When Billie Jean began her career in tennis, she was considered an amateur player—as was any player who wished to compete in the prestigious Grand Slam tournaments. Officially, these players received no prize money. When Billie Jean and Karen Hantze won their Wimbledon doubles title in 1961, the dominating duo was too impoverished to attend the traditional Wimbledon ball! Instead, they ate a spaghetti dinner, courtesy of sportswriter Bud Collins. The first time Billie Jean won the Wimbledon singles title—then considered

Billie Jean King (*left*) and Rosie Casals, shown winning the 1973 Wimbledon final, formed a great doubles team.

the championship of the world—her "prize" was six Mars bars, left in her hotel room by her fellow players.

Players received reimbursement for travel expenses, but that was it—at least in theory. In truth, however, some tournament directors paid top players under the table—a situation that led the legendary Arthur Ashe to declare, "We all deserve Oscars for impersonating amateurs." Billie Jean agreed, referring to this practice as "shamateurism." But even the players who received this illegal booty weren't likely to grow rich. Billie Jean herself claimed that the most money she ever made as an amateur was $7,000, in 1967. That year, she won the singles, doubles, and mixed doubles titles at both Wimbledon and the US Championships.

Besides, it was all terribly disillusioning. "Everything was such a sham," Billie Jean recalled. "Imagine being a kid, still in your teens, and dickering over the phone with some tournament director for under-the-table appearance money and then arriving, to be greeted with an envelope full of cash." She continued, "It was such a penny-ante form of soul-selling."

Billie Jean began speaking openly about her frustration with the tennis establishment. Something had to change— and finally, thanks in part to Billie Jean's efforts, it did. The year 1968 marked the beginning of the so-called **Open Era**, in which professionals and amateurs were permitted to play in Grand Slam and other prestigious tournaments in the hopes of earning prize money.

Billie Jean was thrilled. She and three other female players—Rosie Casals, Francoise Durr, and Ann Jones—

immediately turned pro, joining the now-defunct National Tennis League alongside male players Ken Rosewall, Roy Emerson, Pancho Gonzales, and Rod Laver. They became, in Billie Jean's words, "the only women tennis professionals in the world who actually earned our money by playing."

Dealing with Injury

In September 1968, Billie Jean underwent surgery to repair cartilage in her left knee. This was a major surgery, involving a week's hospital stay, a straight cast, and almost a year of recovery. The long-term prognosis was grim. "My doctor told me, 'Don't count on ever playing Wimbledon again,'" Billie Jean said.

The doctor was wrong. King returned to professional play in May 1969. She won the Irish Open for the second time as well as the Pacific Coast Pro, the Los Angeles Pro, and the South African Open. She did not win a single Grand Slam title that year, but she said the problem wasn't her left knee. Rather, she had developed a painful case of tennis elbow. Nevertheless, she said, "I expect to have a real big year in 1970."

She didn't: her 1970 season was less than stellar. Although she managed to win a few tournaments, she lost her number one ranking. It was reclaimed by Court, who won all four Grand Slam singles titles that year. Worse, Billie Jean was again plagued by injury—this time in her right knee. In July of that year, she underwent surgery again.

Fighting Back

In 1971, things turned around. Billie Jean reclaimed the world number one ranking, although she was again forced to share the honor—this time with Australian player Evonne Goolagong Cawley. She won only one Grand Slam singles title that year—the US Championships, which had by then become the US Open—but claimed seventeen singles titles in all.

In 1972, she was again number one—and this time, she didn't have to share the ranking. Indeed, King dominated the women's circuit, claiming three Grand Slam singles titles, including the French Open, and winning six consecutive tournaments during the summer months. Interestingly, 1972 was also a significant year for Billie Jean's brother, R.J. He made his Major League Baseball debut on June 11 of that year, pitching for the San Francisco Giants. He would go on to play in the Major Leagues until 1983.

In 1973, it was Margaret Court's turn. Court, who had been absent from the tour for most of the previous year following the birth of her first child, won three Grand Slam singles titles and reclaimed the top spot. Still, King won Wimbledon as well as several other tournaments, securing her spot as the world's number two player.

Taking a Stand for Equal Pay

Billie Jean had enjoyed tremendous success on the court, but in her view, she had not been compensated fairly. Indeed, none of the female players had been. The fact was, when it came to prize money for professional tennis players, men and women were treated very differently. For example, in 1968, the men's singles champion at Wimbledon, Rod Laver, received $4,800 in prize money. The women's singles champion, Billie Jean, earned just $1,800. Similarly, in 1970, male player Ilie Năstase received $3,500 for winning the Italian Open. The women's champion—again Billie Jean—earned just $600. Worse, when Margaret Court won a Grand Slam in 1970—in other words, she won all four Grand Slam singles tournaments in a single calendar year—she received a mere $15,000 bonus. In contrast, men could receive up to $1 million! At the same time, the number of tournaments for women was quickly shrinking.

Fed up, Billie Jean—with her husband Larry's support—took a stand. She said, "Promoters were making more money. Male tennis players were making more money. Everybody was making more money except the women." In 1971, she rallied eight other top female players to her cause. This group was dubbed the Original Nine. The group approached the men about joining forces, but the men said no. Next, the group went to the US Lawn Tennis Association (USLTA), the sport's governing body in the United States, about forming a woman's tour, in the hopes that would equalize pay. "They also refused," said Billie Jean. She continued, "At that point, we knew that if we were ever going to be treated as equals, we were going to have to do it by—and for—ourselves."

SCORECARD

Career singles titles: 129 titles won, 62 as an amateur and 67 on the pro tour, in 183 finals appearances.

Grand Slam titles: Thirty-nine total titles, including twelve in singles, sixteen in doubles, and eleven in mixed doubles. Among them are a record twenty at Wimbledon including two "Wimbledon triples" (winning singles, doubles, and mixed doubles in the same year).

Pro career record: 695–155 in singles, and 87–37 in doubles.

Years ranked number one in the world: Six years, 1966–1968, 1971–1972, and 1974.

Federation Cup record: Overall, 52-4, with a 26-3 mark in singles and 26-1 in doubles. She won three titles as a player (1963, 1966-67) and four as a captain (1977-79 and 1996).

Honors and achievements: First woman to win $100,000 in prize money in one calendar year ($117,000 in 1971); winner of the Battle of the Sexes against Bobby Riggs, 1973; first president of the Women's Tennis Association; first female commissioner of a professional sports league (World Team Tennis); Associated Press Female Athlete of the Year, 1967 and 1973; *Sports Illustrated* Sportswoman of the Year (first time a woman was so honored), 1972; Inducted into the Women's Sports Hall of Fame,1980, the International Tennis Hall of Fame, 1987, and the National Women's Hall of Fame, 1990; captain of US Olympic team, 1996 and 2000; Arthur Ashe Award for Courage, 1999; United States Tennis Association renames National Tennis Center as Billie Jean King National Tennis Center, 2006; Presidential Medal of Freedom recipient, 2009.

One member of the Original Nine was Julie Heldman. Her mother, Gladys Heldman, was the publisher of *World Tennis* magazine. The Original Nine enlisted Gladys to negotiate for higher prize money on the group's behalf. The USLTA opposed the group's efforts, but the women felt it had to be done.

Gladys Heldman took aim at the Pacific Southwest Championships. This popular tournament, held in Los Angeles, paid male players a whopping eight times more prize money than their female counterparts. Male players could earn $12,000, while the women were limited to $1,500. Heldman asked tournament director Jack Kramer, a former player, to even the purses—or at least give the women 25 percent. He refused. In response, the Original Nine, risking expulsion from the USLTA, boycotted the tournament. Each woman signed a symbolic $1 contract with Heldman to play at their own competition, the Houston Women's Invitational, complete with a $7,500 purse. This tournament would, in Billie Jean's own words, "forever change tennis and open the doors for generations of women professional tennis players to make a living playing the sport they love."

The Houston Women's Invitational would become the first event in a new women's tour, sponsored by Virginia Slims, a brand of cigarette aimed at women. Despite its connection with tobacco, known to cause cancer, King promoted the tour vigorously. By the end of the 1970s, the independent Virginia Slims Series would grow to eight venues, with forty players, despite the USLTA's refusal to

The Original Nine were honored at the Family Circle Cup in 2012, forty years after they started the women's pro tour. They are, from left: Billie Jean King, Jane "Peaches" Bartkowicz, Kristy Pigeon, Valerie Ziegenfuss, Judy Tegart Dalton, Julie Heldman, Kerry Melville Reid, Nancy Richey, and Rosie Casals.

sanction it. In 1971, it grew even more, boasting nineteen tournaments and a total purse of $309,100. By 1973, the series offered twenty-two tournaments and $775,000 in prize money. As King observed, "Women's tennis players made greater gains in the three years between 1970 and 1973 than in the thirty previous years combined."

Later that same year, the USLTA saw the error in its ways, and agreed to merge its women's tour with the Virginia Slims Series. Even more amazing, with the backing of the USLTA, the US Open became the first major tournament to offer equal prize money to men and women. While it would be some time before all four Grand Slams offered equal pay—Wimbledon would not offer equal prize money until 2007—it was a start.

The year 1973 marked one more significant development: Billie Jean pushed for the formation of a players' union, called the Women's Tennis Association (WTA). As noted by author Susan Ware in her book on King, "The need for an organization to stand up for women's interests and speak in a unified voice seemed like a no-brainer to King." The other players weren't so sure. King brought them around, however—by locking them in a room at the Hotel Gloucester in London until they all agreed to join. The WTA eventually morphed into the premiere women's professional tennis tour. It would become, in its own words, "the global leader in women's professional sport, with more than 2,500 players representing 92 nations competing for a record $129 million in prize money at the WTA's 55 events and four Grand Slams in 33 countries."

King was rewarded for her stand for equal pay. In 1971, she became the first female athlete to earn more than $100,000 in a single year. ("From a blunt point of view," King said later, winning $100,000 "was no big deal—Rod Laver made $292,000 on the men's tour that same year.") In 1973, Billie Jean's earnings climbed to an estimated $500,000. Still, compared to female players in the years that followed, her earnings were relatively paltry.

As one reporter noted in 1999, King "has made more money than anyone else. Sadly, for Billie Jean, of course, the money was not made by her personally, but rather by the generations of women tennis players who emerged after she had spent a decade roughing up the authorities in the battle for equality of status and reward." Serena Williams alone has won $72 million in prize money during the course of her career. Her sister Venus has likewise become very rich, earning some $30 million. Those figures are at least in part due to King's considerable efforts on behalf of female players. "Today's young women—in tennis and in general—aren't just hoping to be treated fairly and equally, they expect it," King said. "Their sense of entitlement and equality reinforces my own."

To King, her efforts weren't just about equal pay for female players. "The money's fine," she said, "but everyone's talked about the money so much they forget what the purpose was, for me anyway." She explained: "The purpose is to enable women to play and to make people pay attention."

Bobby Riggs, pictured circa 1940, was small but successful because of ball control, cunning, and foot speed.

CHAPTER 3

AN OFFER KING *COULD* REFUSE

"Billie Jean was too good, too quick."

—Bobby Riggs

I n 1973, King received an offer that, at first, she *could* refuse. It came from Robert "Bobby" Larimore Riggs, an American tennis player who had been the world number one for three years during the 1930s and 1940s. Riggs, a self-proclaimed "male chauvinist pig," had come out of retirement at the age of fifty-five and had challenged King to a match. He believed—or in any case *said* he believed—that the women's game was "inferior," and that even at his advanced age, he could beat any of the top female players. Billie Jean, busy playing the Virginia Slims Series, declined. Soon, however, events would persuade her to change her mind, and to play in one of the biggest tennis matches in the history of the sport.

Like Billie Jean, Bobby Riggs was from Southern California, and like Billie Jean, he first picked up a tennis racket at the age of eleven. Riggs had even had run-ins with "Mr. Tennis of the West Coast" Perry T. Jones, as Billie Jean did. In his autobiography, Riggs accused Jones of refusing to help him because he was too small. (Another player, Jack Kramer, disputed this, noting that Jones turned against Riggs because Riggs was "a kid hustler.")

To be fair, Riggs *was* small. To compensate, he relied entirely on speed, ball control, and cunning. Soon, he began winning tournaments. By the age of sixteen, he was the fifth-ranked junior player in America. By the age of eighteen, he'd climbed to the number four spot in the US men's rankings.

Kramer said of Riggs that he "could keep the ball in play, and he could find ways to control the bigger, more powerful opponent." Kramer continued, "He could pin you back by hitting long, down the lines, and then he'd run you ragged with chips and **drop shots**. He was outstanding with a volley from either side, and he could **lob** as well as any man. … He could also lob on the run. He could disguise it, and he could hit winning overheads. They weren't powerful, but they were always on target."

In 1939, at the age of twenty-one, Riggs captured the Wimbledon triple, winning the singles, doubles, and mixed doubles titles. (This was a feat that Billie Jean herself would achieve twice, in 1967 and 1973.) Riggs's victory was made even sweeter by the $500 bet he had placed on himself before the tournament, which yielded a $105,000 payoff—equivalent to $1,780,000 today. He also won the US Championships that year—an accomplishment he would repeat the following year—and garnered the world number one ranking. Riggs's tennis career was interrupted by World War II, during which he served in the US Navy.

WOMEN'S LIB

Bobby Riggs's chauvinistic persona was in large part in response to a growing women's movement called women's liberation, or women's lib. Women's lib was considered the "second wave" of feminism. (The "first wave" of feminism culminated with the passage of the Nineteenth Amendment to the US Constitution in 1920, which guaranteed women the right to vote.) Second-wave feminism, which began during the early 1960s and continued through the late 1980s, focused on equal rights and on women's autonomy over their own bodies.

Women's liberation meant many different things to many different people. To Billie Jean King, it meant that "every woman ought to be able to pursue whatever career or personal lifestyle she chooses as a full and equal member of society without fear of discrimination." In discussing the movement, King often reminded listeners that, "Back in 1973 a woman could not even get a credit card without her husband cosigning."

In time, King would become closely associated in the public's mind with the women's movement, but King despised labels. She didn't want to be pegged as a so-called "feminist," "women's libber," or, as some people called her, "women's lobber"—a play on the word *lob*, a type of tennis shot. Frankly, all King wanted was to ensure equal pay for female tennis players. Soon, however, she began to understand her role in the larger struggle for women's rights. "Because of my prominence, or notoriety, or whatever you want to call it, I've got a platform," she said, according to the book *Game, Set, Match: Billie Jean King and the Revolution in Women's Sports*. "I'm in a position to be heard out." She continued, "There are certainly a lot of women who are more intelligent than I am and better informed about things like women's liberation, for example, but they can't reach anybody. What I have and what they don't have, simply, is a forum." King would learn to use this forum to her advantage, and to the advantage of women everywhere.

After the war, he resumed play, turning professional in 1946. In 1946, 1947, and 1949, Riggs won the US Pro Title, establishing himself once again as the best player in the world.

Riggs retired from professional play in 1951, but he never gave up tennis altogether, playing against seniors and amateurs at clubs across the country. Often, he placed wagers on his games. He was, in his own words, a "hustler." Billie Jean agreed with that assessment, adding "motormouth" to the description.

In the early 1970s, during the height of the women's movement, it occurred to Riggs that he could make some easy money by competing against top female players in exhibition matches. In February 1973, Riggs held a press conference at a San Diego hotel. "No woman who ever lived could compete with a man on an equal basis," he said, adding, "Even a fifty-five-year-old man like me." He then waved a cashier's check in the air, offering it to Margaret Court, young up-and-comer Chris Evert, or Billie Jean King. Chris Evert and Billie Jean declined the offer. Margaret Court, on the other hand, accepted it.

Riggs Versus Court

On May 13, 1973—Mother's Day—Bobby Riggs and Margaret Court met across the net. Court, then thirty years old and at the top of her game, was certain she would win. After all, how could she—how could *anyone*—take Riggs seriously? He was just a mouthy old man. To Court, the

Bobby Riggs flashes the two $5,000 checks he won by defeating Margaret Court in the winner-take-all "Mother's Day Massacre."

match against Riggs represented an easy payday—nothing else. The purse for the winner-take-all event was $10,000.

Not even Riggs's sexist statements about the inferiority of the women's game raised Court's ire. In spite of her unusual success as a female athlete, Court didn't identify with the growing women's movement. She was more traditional—a proud wife and mother. She failed to recognize what was at stake. Court saw the game as nothing more than an easy way to earn a few thousand dollars, but it was much more than that. The fact was, the credibility of the women's game—indeed, of the entire women's movement—was on the line. Still, Margaret declared, "I am not carrying the banner for women's lib."

King told the *New York Times* for an article published on August 21, 2005, that Court informed her during an elevator ride in Detroit that she was going to play Riggs. King told the newspaper their conversation went this way:

When Court said she was going to earn $10,000, King replied, "That's not enough, and, secondly, this is not about tennis."

Court responded, "What do you mean? I'm about to get $10,000."

"Margaret, I'm just going to ask one thing of you: You have to win this match." When Court nodded politely, King added, "No, I mean it. You have to win this match. You have no idea how important this is."

"Margaret didn't see the big picture," King said later. "She just didn't get it."

Bobby Riggs consoles Margaret Court after routing her at Ramona, California, on May 13, 1973.

Court may not have taken the match seriously, but Riggs certainly did. "For three or four months, we're talking running every day, playing six hours of tennis a day," recalled his son, Larry. "He was playing the best tennis of his life." Riggs even gave up alcohol. What's more, he scouted Court on the Virginia Slims circuit, taking notes about her style of play. He quickly devised a plan to defeat her. Rather than play a power game, he would keep her off balance with drop shots, lobs, spins, and other soft shots. "I'm just going to destroy her," Riggs told his son. Riggs was right. In just fifty-seven minutes, Riggs won the match. The final score: an embarrassing 6–2, 6–1. It was a result that became known as "The Mother's Day Massacre."

"I played extremely well that match, and she, of course, was off her game and just couldn't seem to get her act together," said Riggs afterward. Later, Court would say, "Sometimes I look back and think, 'Why did I need to do it?'" She added, "We all make mistakes in life. That was one of my mistakes."

For her part, Billie Jean was distraught. She knew that Riggs's victory meant more than just Court's humiliation. It undercut her efforts to ensure equal pay for men and women in tennis and weakened the women's movement as a whole. She had to do something. "That's it," twenty-nine-year-old Billie Jean said to herself, "I've got to play him."

CONSERVATIVE MARGARET COURT

Australian tennis phenomenon Margaret Court did not view herself as "carrying the banner for women's lib." Indeed, despite the opportunities she'd enjoyed and her tremendous success in tennis, Margaret was about as far from a women's libber as a person could be.

Margaret was deeply religious. Although she was raised as a Roman Catholic, she converted to Pentecostalism in the mid-1970s. Pentecostalism is a form of Protestant Christianity that views the Bible as the absolute, inerrant truth and believes in adult baptism and in the use of spiritual gifts such as divine healing and speaking in tongues. As such, Margaret viewed the women's movement with deep skepticism, as its philosophy appeared to be counter to that of the Bible.

In 1991, long after her playing career was over, Margaret became a minister, later founding her own ministry, called Margaret Court Ministries. In 1995, she founded a Pentecostal church in Perth, Australia, called Victory Life Centre. For years, she hosted her own television show, *A Life of Victory*, on the Australian Christian Channel.

Court has long been an outspoken opponent of homosexuality. Her views would be condemned by several prominent figures in the tennis world, including Billie Jean King.

The Challenge

"Now, I want King bad," Riggs told the press. "I'll play her on clay, grass, wood, cement, marble, or roller skates." This time, Billie Jean—the "women's libber leader," according to Riggs—accepted the challenge. As she explained, "If I won, it might get the minds and hearts of Americans to begin to match up on issues of equality." The match was on.

Scheduled for September 20, 1973, at the Houston Astrodome, it was called the "Battle of the Sexes." To sweeten the pot, promoters offered a $100,000 winner-take-all prize. But for Billie Jean, the money was secondary. She was much more concerned about the social implications of the match. "I thought it would set us back fifty years if I didn't win that match," she said in *Billie Jean*. "It would ruin the women's [tennis] tour and affect all women's self-esteem."

Predictably, Riggs mouthed off incessantly in the months leading up to the match. "Personally," he said during one press conference, "I would wish that the women would stay in the home and do the kitchen work and take care of the baby." He continued, "It's a big mistake for them to get mixed up in these mixed-sex matches." It was as though he was determined to be as offensive as possible. (Interestingly, Riggs's son Larry later insisted this was all an act. He claimed his father was not a chauvinist, and that he viewed women as equals—and this may well have been the case. Indeed, Riggs's first tennis coach was a woman, Eleanor "Teach" Tennant.)

"The hype never really stopped," King recalled in *Billie Jean*. "If it started to slow down, Bobby would whip it back up again." But King kept quiet. "I tried not to get too caught up with Bobby's histrionics," she said. "He was spouting his male-chauvinistic propaganda to anyone who would listen—in television interviews, newspapers, magazines, you name it. I just laughed it off."

And of course, she trained. "I knew if I didn't prepare specifically for this match," Billie Jean said, "I would be in trouble. So I did absolutely everything I could to prepare." She continued, "I was painfully aware that if I lost, it could set women's sports and women's rights issues back significantly."

First, she needed to prepare physically. The Battle of the Sexes would be a five-set match, whereas matches on the women's circuit were three sets. So Billie Jean needed to make sure she would have enough stamina to go the distance. Of course, she also needed to prepare a strategy to win. To that end, Billie Jean carefully studied Riggs's match with Court. At first, she planned to simply end each point as quickly as she could. But then she realized that she could use Riggs's age against him by keeping him running. "I would get him into long rallies, back and forth, early in the match, still going to the net when it made sense but running him as much as possible," she said.

In contrast, Riggs did little to prepare. Perhaps overconfident after his match with Court, Riggs spent the weeks leading up to the Battle of the Sexes drinking, carousing, and generally stirring things up. He barely picked up his racket. Still, on the night before the match, he assured a friend, "There's no way that broad can beat me," referring to King. Riggs's son Larry was less confident. "You're going to embarrass yourself," he told Riggs before the match.

Perhaps unaware of Riggs's poor preparation, the public found it hard to believe that King could prevail. Before the match, tennis greats Pancho Gonzales, John Newcombe, and Chris Evert predicted that Riggs would win. ("I was such an idiot," Evert would say later. "I've changed since.") Likewise, the line in Las Vegas favored Riggs. "King money is scarce," observed sports commentator Jimmy the Greek. "It's hard to find a bet on the girl." King had to prove them wrong.

The Match

The match was unlike any Billie Jean had played in before. Put simply, it was a spectacle, not unlike the circus. Billie Jean, wearing a blue-and-white sequined tennis dress conceived by Ted Tinling—a fashion designer who was a mainstay on the women's tennis circuit and had designed daring dresses for stars such as Billie Jean, Martina Navratilova, Chris Evert, and others—entered the arena like an Egyptian queen. She perched, in her words, on "a gaudy, gold gilt Egyptian litter with feathers coming out of the top of the chair," carried by four bare-chested men, all members of the Rice University

There was a circus atmosphere in the Houston Astrodome for the Battle of the Sexes. Billie Jean King arrived and departed on a litter carried by college athletes.

men's track and field team. "I had only one real problem with the whole scene," recalled King: "I'm afraid of heights! I thought they were going to drop me." Riggs was carted in on a golden rickshaw, pulled by six young models in red and gold outfits, whom he called "Bobby's Bosom Buddies."

More than thirty thousand fans were in attendance—to this day, the largest crowd ever at a tennis match in the United States. Among them were several celebrities such as singer Andy Williams, actors Lee Majors and Farrah Fawcett, and musician Glen Campbell. And incredibly, ninety million more worldwide watched on TV.

Before the match, Riggs presented Billie Jean with a gigantic lollipop. "Billie Jean is going to be a sucker for my wiles tonight," he said over the loudspeaker. "So I brought her the biggest sucker I could find." For her part, Billie Jean presented Riggs with a live piglet—his very own "chauvinist pig."

Billie Jean knew that to win, she would need to take the first set. "I needed the psychological advantage," she explained. But in the fifth game, Riggs broke her serve. Suddenly, she was down 3–2. She had to regain control—and she did. "Bobby's technique"—the same one he had used with Margaret Court—"was to put a lot of spin on the ball and not much behind it, which meant that I would have to supply all of the power," recalled Billie Jean. "I decided to put it back to him by hitting the ball softly and all over the court."

Billie Jean Kings exults after closing out her must-win match against Bobby Riggs.

According to King, "It worked like a charm." Riggs quickly became winded. Billie Jean said, "Within minutes, he was covered in sweat." Riggs made several unforced errors. He hit balls into the net. He double-faulted at key moments. "He was in slow motion," remembered Donald Dell, a former Davis Cup captain and one of the first professional sports agents. "It was as if he had taken a sleeping pill." Lornie Kuhle, a close friend of Riggs's, said, "It was like Bobby finally realized that the final exam was here and he hadn't studied for it." Famed TV announcer Howard Cosell observed, "Funny. With this match I guess we all expected some high humor involved in it. Instead, it's become a very serious, serious thing." Cosell added, "The comedy has gone out of Bobby Riggs."

Billie Jean won the first set, 6–4. She then claimed the second and third sets, 6–3. She had won the match without dropping a set. An ecstatic King tossed her racket into the air.

The *London Sunday Times* cleverly called her victory "the drop shot and volley heard around the world." One *New York Times* writer concurred, noting that King "convinced skeptics that a female athlete can survive pressure-filled situations and that men are as susceptible to nerves as women." Another *New York Times* writer noted, "In a single tennis match, Billie Jean King was able to do more for the cause of women than most feminists can achieve in a lifetime." *Sports Illustrated* called King's performance "a classic example of a skilled athlete performing at peak efficiency in the most important moment of her life." Journalist Grace Lichtenstein proclaimed Billie Jean "a national folk heroine—an athletic Eleanor Roosevelt."

Riggs was a surprisingly gracious loser. Though visibly drained, he jumped the net to congratulate King. "I underestimated you," he told her. They walked off the court arm in arm. Later, she would say of Riggs, "He acted like a true gentleman when the match was done, he behaved with integrity, and he was a great sport."

After the match, Riggs told reporters, "Billie Jean was too good, too quick. I know I said a lot of things she made me eat tonight. I guess I'm the biggest bum of all time now. But I have to take it."

Later, a humiliated Riggs retreated to his room at the AstroWorld Hotel. Shivering in an ice bath after the match, he even thought about drowning himself. Later, Riggs would tell his son Larry that his match with Billie Jean was "the worst thing I've ever done." According to his friends, he remained depressed for months after the match.

Sour Grapes?

After King beat Riggs, some people claimed the match had been rigged. Many believed that Riggs had bet money against himself and lost the match on purpose. There were even rumors that Riggs owed money to the Mafia, and that he threw the match to cancel those debts. Of course,

Billie Jean King and Bobby Riggs remained friends after the Battle of the Sexes, even taking part in a celebrity tennis match in 1993.

beneath all these claims was the assumption that a woman could never beat a man in an athletic contest.

King was unmoved. "A lot of people, men particularly, don't like it if a woman wins," she said. "They make up stories." Besides, she added, it "was not really in Bobby's best interest in any way to lose that match."

Even Jack Kramer—no friend of King's—agreed. (Kramer was the tournament director of the Pacific Southwest Championships who had refused the Original Nine's plea for equal pay. Although he was originally slated by ABC as a commentator for the Battle of the Sexes, Billie Jean demanded they drop him. "He doesn't believe in women's tennis. Why should he be part of this match? Either he goes, or I go.") "A lot of men—especially around our age—were so stunned when he lost that they figured he must have tanked," Kramer said. "But what motive would Riggs have had for that? Bobby Riggs, the biggest ham in the world, gets his great audience—and purposefully looks bad? There's no way." Besides, said Kramer, "If he had beaten Billie Jean, he could have kept the act going indefinitely."

Riggs himself later denied that he had thrown the match. "People said I was tanking," he told one journalist in 1995. "But Billie Jean beat me fair and square. I tried as hard as I could, but I made the classic mistake of overestimating myself and underestimating Billie Jean. I didn't really think she had a chance."

Riggs even took a public lie detector test to put an end to the rumor that he had thrown the match—and passed.

A Lasting Friendship

"Even though we had a rivalry on the court," Billie Jean said of Bobby Riggs, "we truly did like each other." In the years after the match, their friendship grew. They even appeared on a TV show called *The Odd Couple* together. "The script called for Bobby and me to play table tennis against each other," Billie Jean recalled.

Riggs's love for tennis never died. He won numerous national titles as a senior player in his sixties and seventies.

Before Riggs died in October of 1995, Billie Jean called him to say goodbye. She offered to visit him, but he declined; he didn't want her to see him in his diminished condition. Interestingly, Riggs had long since put his chauvinistic views—if, indeed, he had ever actually held them—aside. "Well, we did it," he said to King, referring to the Battle of the Sexes and its importance to society as a whole. "We really made a difference, didn't we?" Before Billie Jean hung up, she said, "I love you." "I love you," Riggs said back.

The Cleveland Nets attracted two top male players, Bjorn Borg (*left*) and Marty Riessen, as well as Borg's girlfriend Mariana Simionescu (*right*), in 1977.

CHAPTER 4
EXPANDING HER WORLD

"I couldn't get in a closet deep enough."

—Billie Jean King

B illie Jean King had a banner year in 1973. She won Wimbledon singles, doubles, and mixed doubles titles—a so-called "Wimbledon triple." She won the US Open mixed doubles. She won eight other singles tournaments. She was instrumental in the formation of the WTA. She was named female athlete of the year by the Associated Press. And of course, she defeated Bobby Riggs in the Battle of the Sexes.

The next year, 1974, King's success on the court continued. She won five of the first seven tournaments she played. She was also the US Open singles and doubles champion. However, other important milestones were reached that year. One was the debut of World Team Tennis, which was the brainchild of King and her husband, Larry. World Team Tennis—WTT for short—was, in the words of author Susan Ware, "a new venture designed to break out tennis from its country-club setting and make it into a popular team sport on par with baseball, football, or basketball." Billie Jean put it this way: "The biggest sports in the world are team sports, and I want to make tennis huge."

Each World Team Tennis team boasted at least two men and two women, each with an equal role in the squad's success. For King, this was perhaps the most compelling aspect of the league. "In Team Tennis, if you help your teammate—it doesn't matter which gender—then everybody wins," she said, adding, "That's the kind of teamwork I want to see happen in the business world, in marriage, and everything."

World Team Tennis had an unusual format. Athletes played in matches that consisted of five sets, with each set featuring a different configuration—men's singles, men's doubles, women's singles, women's doubles, and mixed doubles. The first player or team to win five games won the set.

Unlike with traditional tennis, in World Team Tennis, it was not necessary to win a set by two games. Similarly, it was not necessary to win a game by two points. If players were tied at 40–40, whoever won the next point won the game. The same went for the tiebreaker that took effect when players were tied 4–4 in a set: whoever won the next point won the set. "Of course the pressure [was] excruciating," Billie Jean said of the format, which did not allow for second chances the way traditional tennis does. "But every athlete, in every sport, should have to face that now-or-never moment at some point."

Attending a WTT match was a completely different experience from going to a traditional tennis tournament. In a traditional tournament, officials call for complete quiet during play. At WTT events, fans were encouraged to yell, scream, and even boo players. "Polite applause at tennis matches is ridiculous," observed King.

Initially, there were sixteen franchises, including the Boston Lobsters, the Chicago Aces, the Denver Racquets, the Los Angeles Strings, the New York Sets, and the Philadelphia Freedom. Team owners lured top players with lucrative contracts, including Rod Laver, Björn Borg, Chris Evert, John McEnroe, Jimmy Connors, Martina Navratilova, and, of course, King, who served as a player and the coach of the Philadelphia Freedom before being traded to the New York Sets.

The league got a promotion boost in 1975 when singer and pianist Elton John released a single called "Philadelphia Freedom." The song, composed by John and his long-time colleague Bernie Taupin, was written for King. In addition to burning up the pop and R&B charts—it would quickly claim the number one spot in both—the song served as the anthem for King's World Team Tennis team. The singer and the tennis player had met in 1973 and become fast friends. John often attended matches, even going so far as to dress in the Freedom uniform and sit on the bench, and when Elton went on tour, Billie Jean attended his concerts. "Elton would even get me up on the stage as a BV—a backup vocalist," Billie Jean remembered. "I was a real Elton groupie for a while."

Attendance at the matches was not sufficient to cover the salaries of the top players. The number of teams quickly

Billie Jean King and fellow tennis star Andre Agassi joined longtime friend Elton John at an Elton John AIDS Foundation fundraiser in 2004.

dwindled from sixteen to eleven to nine. By the end of 1978, the league was, to quote Susan Ware, "basically kaput." Eight of the remaining nine teams folded, but Billie Jean and Larry didn't give up. In 1981, they rebooted the league, which fluctuated between four and twelve teams. In 1985, Billie Jean became league commissioner—the first female commissioner of a professional sports league ever—a post she would hold until 2001. In 2015, there were still seven World Team Tennis teams, including Billie Jean's beloved Philadelphia Freedom.

Although King is no longer commissioner of the league, it remains close to her heart. In fact, according to the *Washington Post*, "Of all the things icon Billie Jean King has accomplished in tennis, helping found the World Team Tennis league is at the top of the list. It's more important to her than starting the Women's Tennis Association, and winning thirty-nine Grand Slam singles, doubles and mixed doubles titles."

Magazine Mogul

Another major milestone for King was the unveiling of *womenSports* magazine. The idea for the publication stemmed from a conversation that Billie Jean and Larry King had had the year before. When Billie Jean complained about the lack of coverage of female athletes in *Sports Illustrated*, Larry responded by suggesting she start a magazine of her own. And thus, *womenSports* was born.

Neither Billie Jean nor Larry knew the first thing about running a magazine. As Billie Jean put it, "We didn't know a byline from a center spread." But Billie Jean believed that publishing *womenSports* was an absolute necessity. "No one knows women athletes as personalities," Billie Jean told the *Wall Street Journal*. "Women athletes need a vehicle to communicate with others as well as themselves." In Billie Jean's view, *womenSports* would do just that. "My hope is that through *womenSports*, many more women will take pride in their performance in sports," she wrote in the magazine's first issue, released in June 1974.

The magazine, described as "glossy" and "upbeat," covered a variety of sports, introducing readers to top athletes and teams. Naturally, given King's involvement in the magazine, tennis was well represented, but *womenSports* also covered such sports as basketball, field hockey, running, soccer, softball, skiing, surfing, and volleyball. Female athletes from days gone by were given their due in a regular feature cleverly called "Foremothers."

Circulation and revenues were good enough to keep the magazine going until 1978.

Women's Sports Foundation

Billie Jean King once observed, "Whereas male athletes are celebrated so in our society, female athletes are hardly treated with the same honor." To rectify that, Billie Jean formed the Women's Sports Foundation in 1974. A nonprofit national organization, the WSF is, in Billie

Jean's own words, "dedicated to encouraging women of all ages and all skill levels to participate in sports activities for health, enjoyment, and development."

The goals of the organization were and remain fourfold. As noted by author Susan Ware in her book on King, they are as follows:

- To educate women and the general public with respect to women in sports and women's athletic capabilities and achievements

- To promote equal rights and opportunities for women in sports and to educate women in sports and the general public as to discrimination against women in sports

- To educate and support women in increasing their athletic good sportsmanship and fair play

- To encourage and support the participation of women in sports for their health, enjoyment and career opportunities

First on the WSF's agenda was "to change society's attitudes." As noted by Billie Jean at an early meeting of the foundation, "There are still negative ideas and prejudices flowing around about women in sports." As part of its strategy to achieve this, the foundation sought and received the support of several prominent female athletes, including Donna de Varona (swimming), Suzy Chaffee (alpine skiing), Wyomia Tyus (track and field), Dianne

Billie Jean (*center*) presented the Sportswoman of the Year Team Sport Award to ice dancer Meryl Davis (*second from left*) at the 2014 Women's Sports Foundation's thirty-fifth Annual Salute to Women In Sports. King was joined by skater Michelle Kwan (*left*), Davis's ice dance partner Charlie White, and snowboarder Amy Purdy.

Holum (speed skating), Micki King (diving), Joan Joyce (softball), Jane Blalock (golf), Paula Sperber (bowling), Mary Jo Peppler (volleyball), Chris Evert (tennis), and of course, Billie Jean. Together, these women—and many more who came after—worked to change society's attitudes about female athletes.

The WSF also revived Billie Jean's *womenSports* magazine, although the publication was renamed slightly to *Women's Sports*. It served as both the magazine for members of the WSF and as a general publication to encourage "more and more women to discover for themselves the added dimensions that participation in active sports can bring to their lives."

More than forty years later, the WSF is still going strong, although its publication, *Women's Sports*, eventually ceased operation. Current WSF CEO Deborah Slaner Larkin notes, "We believe that sports are a birthright and we use our powerful voice to advocate for equality in sports for every girl and woman. We speak out for safe, equal playing fields for school-aged and elite athletes around the world and promote female leadership in all areas of sports."

A New Cause

Near the end of her professional tennis career, Billie Jean became associated with a new cause—albeit unwillingly. That cause was lesbian/gay/bisexual/transgender (LGBT) rights. In 1981, it was revealed that Billie Jean had conducted an affair with a woman. The woman in question was Marilyn Barnett, who had been Billie Jean's secretary. Marilyn sued Billie Jean for palimony, which, according to *Merriam-Webster Dictionary*, is "a court-ordered allowance paid by one member of a couple formerly living together out of wedlock to the other." Ultimately, Barnett lost her case. Billie Jean was not required to pay palimony, but the damage—both personal and professional—had been done.

From a personal standpoint, there was the damage to Billie Jean and Larry's relationship. The couple would eventually divorce six years later, after twenty-two years of marriage. Billie Jean also felt a deep shame. "Growing up, I was conditioned to be leery of homosexuals," she said. This view came in large part from her father. "He had very strong—and I mean *very* strong—feelings about homosexuals," Billie Jean recalled.

Barnett's revelation also caused waves in Billie Jean's professional life. Billie Jean lost $2 million in endorsements within twenty-four hours of the lawsuit being filed. As this income dried up, an aging Billie Jean was forced to keep playing in tournaments just to pay the bills—which, of course, included significant legal fees—and save for the future.

Billie Jean initially sought to play down her homosexuality, even after she was so painfully outed. "I wanted to tell the truth," she said, "but my parents were homophobic," and, she said, "I had people tell me that if I talked about what I was going through, it would be the end of the women's tour." America, she believed, just wasn't ready for a lesbian tennis superstar.

Interestingly, Billie Jean had already spoken up on behalf of another LGBT player: a transgender woman named Renée Richards. In 1976, Richards petitioned the WTA to play as a woman. Initially, several players balked, but not King. "If the doctors say she's a woman, that's good enough for me," she said. "I'll go even further. If Renée thinks she's a woman in her heart and mind, then she is a woman."

One beacon for Billie Jean was the response of the press, which was generally positive. As one reporter for the *Washington Post* wrote, "It should not matter whether she rushed the net as a heterosexual, homosexual, bisexual, or asexual. … What matters is that she plays a swell game of tennis." The reporter went on, "If the tragedy and pain of the Billie Jean King affair does nothing more than put a human face on homosexuality, she will have accomplished quite a bit."

In the end, that's just what happened. Billie Jean put a "human face on homosexuality." But it didn't happen right away. It took Billie Jean time—and "years of therapy"—to accept her sexuality and to be open about it in public. "My sexuality was probably the most difficult struggle I've had in my whole life," she said. "And the one thing it taught me was that until you find your own truth, you really cannot be free."

It helped that the public's views on the issue were also evolving. "In the '70s, there was this huge fear about coming out," Billie Jean said. "It's much better now," she observed in 1997. "In fact, if you want to talk about your sexual orientation, the acceptance level is way up." In time, even Billie Jean's parents accepted her sexuality. "At the age of 51," said Billie Jean, "I was able to talk about it properly with my parents. That was a turning point for me."

King said she did not realize what her sexual orientation was until well after she was married. "I would never have married Larry if I'd known," she told a writer for an online publication. "I never would have done that to him. I was totally in love with Larry when I was twenty-one."

Larry King remarried and had two children with his second wife, Nancy. He said in a 2001 interview that he and Billie Jean remained on good terms, had maintained

Ilana Kloss and Betty Moffitt joined Billie Jean on opening day at the US Open in 2006 at the renamed Billie Jean King National Tennis Center.

business partnerships, and that his ex-wife is his son's godmother.

Today, Billie Jean lives openly with her longtime partner, Ilana Kloss. Ilana, herself a former professional tennis player, hails from South Africa. Billie Jean now feels perfectly comfortable lending her celebrity to various gay causes. She supports the Gay Games, the Gay and Lesbian Alliance Against Defamation (GLAAD), and, of course, the Elton John AIDS Foundation.

These days, Billie Jean is pleased with the progress that's been made with regard to LGBT rights but knows there's still a long road ahead—particularly when it comes to the acceptance of LGBT people in sports. She predicted that only a male superstar—"a gay Michael Jordan"—would overcome resistance to LGBT athletes. "Needless to say," observed author Susan Ware, "this has not yet happened."

Billie Jean Retires

In 1975, Billie Jean was once again Wimbledon singles champion. She defeated Evonne Goolagong Cawley in the second-most lopsided Wimbledon women's final ever: 6–0, 6–1. She called the performance a "near perfect match."

Immediately after her singles win at Wimbledon in 1975, Billie Jean announced her retirement from the women's circuit. "I'm never coming back," she told the press. Billie Jean wanted to leave on a high note. She said,

"I think I've been the most fortunate woman athlete who ever lived up to this time."

It didn't stick, however. "Retiring was the best thing I ever did," Billie Jean said later, "because I learned that I didn't want to be retired." So Billie Jean played on, racking up three more US Open titles (two in doubles and one in mixed doubles), one more Wimbledon title (in doubles), and fifteen more singles titles in various tournaments around the world. Finally, in 1983, one month shy of her fortieth birthday, Billie Jean retired from the women's circuit for good, although she would sporadically play in doubles matches until 1990.

All told, Billie Jean won 129 singles titles over the course of her career, earning a total of $1,966,486 in prize money. Of those 129 singles titles, twelve were Grand Slams. She also won eighty-seven doubles titles, including sixteen Grand Slams, and she won eleven mixed doubles titles, all of which were Grand Slams. She won a **career Grand Slam**—that is, the titles at all four Grand Slam events—in both singles and mixed doubles play. And of course, she achieved her dream of being the number one player in the world.

GAME-CHANGING CHRONOLOGY

1943: Born in Long Beach, California, to Bill and Betty Moffitt.

1954: Learns to play tennis from coach Clyde Walker in the parks of Long Beach.

1958: Wins the Southern California Junior Championships.

1959: Makes her first appearance in a Grand Slam tournament, the US Championships, losing in the first round.

1961: Wins her first Grand Slam doubles title at Wimbledon. Her beloved coach, Clyde Walker, dies the next day.

1965: Marries Larry King; wins Wimbledon doubles title.

1966: Wins first Grand Slam singles title at Wimbledon.

1967: Wins French Championships doubles title, Wimbledon triple (singles, doubles, and mixed doubles), and US Championships singles and mixed doubles titles.

1967: Wins Associated Press Female Athlete of the Year award.

1970: Forms the Original Nine to protest discrepancies in prize money for male and female players, and starts the Virginia Slims Series.

1971: Becomes the first female athlete to surpass $100,000 in prize money in a calendar year.

1972: Wins *Sports Illustrated* Sportsman of the Year award. This marks the first time a female athlete received the award.

1973: Defeats Bobby Riggs in the Battle of the Sexes; forms Women's Tennis Association; wins Associated Press Female Athlete of the Year award for the second time.

1974: Forms World Team Tennis league with her husband Larry; launches *womenSports* magazine; starts Women's Sports Foundation.

1981: "Outed" by former lover Marilyn Barnett.

1983: Retires from tennis. This time, her retirement sticks.

1987: Divorces husband Larry; is inducted into International Tennis Hall of Fame.

1990: Named one of the "100 Most Important Americans of the Twentieth Century" by *Life* magazine.

1999: Receives Arthur Ashe Courage Award.

2006: National Tennis Center renamed the USTA Billie Jean King National Tennis Center.

2009: Receives Presidential Medal of Freedom from President Barack Obama.

Jeanne Moutoussamy Ashe, widow of Arthur Ashe, congratulates Billie Jean after she received the Arthur Ashe Courage Award in 1999.

CHAPTER 5

THE LEGACY OF BILLIE JEAN KING

"American history is full of iconic sports heroes, but until Billie Jean King they were almost exclusively men."

—Author Susan Ware

B illie Jean King is indeed iconic. She has left a tremendous legacy in the sport she loves: tennis. Her mark on the game has been indelible.

Billie Jean was a champion. She won an incredible thirty-nine Grand Slam titles, including twelve singles titles, sixteen doubles titles, and eleven mixed doubles titles. Only two women have won more—Margaret Court (sixty-two) and Martina Navratilova (fifty-six)— although Serena Williams was getting close in 2015 after winning Wimbledon for her twenty-first singles title to go with thirteen doubles titles. Twice, Billie Jean won a "Wimbledon triple," claiming the top prize in singles, doubles, and mixed doubles play. She was the first female athlete to earn more than $100,000 in a calendar year, raking in $117,000 in 1971.

Her old nemesis Margaret Court called Billie Jean "the greatest competitor I've ever known," and her old friend, frequent doubles partner, and member of the Original Nine Rosie Casals observed, "No matter how far down you got her, you could never be sure of beating her." Another member of the Original Nine, Julie Heldman, said, "Billie Jean's the smartest one, the cleverest one you'll ever see. She was the one who was able to channel everything into winning, into being the most consummate tennis player."

King's efforts off the court were even more notable. She spoke up on behalf of all players—men and women alike—who sought to earn a living playing the game. Her agitating helped to usher in the Open Era, in which players could turn professional but continue to play in the world's most prestigious tournaments.

King also spoke up on behalf of female players, whom she believed deserved the same prize money as male players. She and eight other players risked their careers to form the Virginia Slims Series. Soon, many top tournaments began offering equal purses to men and women. Billie Jean was also instrumental in the formation of the Women's Tennis Association, which would grow to serve as a powerful voice for female players.

Of course, King proved once and for all that female athletes were deserving of respect by defeating Bobby Riggs in the Battle of the Sexes. "In the end, I may have beaten Bobby and won the prize money, but that was not the ultimate reward of the match," King said in the book *Pressure Is a Privilege*. "It was getting the validation for women and daughters, implementing social change, getting all people to start thinking differently and work together for equality, and helping others be the best they could be." But, King said, her victory against Riggs "wasn't just for women." She continued, "It was really about both genders." Her win, she believed, caused men "to think differently about things."

Not surprisingly, King's sphere of influence extended beyond just the tennis world. She made a difference for girls and women everywhere—those who played sports and those who didn't. With regard to the latter, basketball player Nancy Lieberman observed, "Billie Jean King never played basketball, but her fingerprints are on the WNBA [Women's National Basketball Association]. Her fingerprints are on women's professional softball, soccer, golf, tennis, and just about any other sport you can think of. She risked her reputation and her career because she believed so strongly that women should have the right to play on and to be part of a team."

Thanks to her victory over Riggs, King "prominently affected the way 50 percent of society thinks and feels about itself," journalist Frank Deford wrote in *Sports Illustrated*. (Deford coauthored a biography of King in 1982.) According to journalist Melissa Murphy, Billie Jean's "fight for equal pay and equal rights for girls and women resonated with a generation during the 1970s and beyond." Martina Navratilova agreed. "She was a crusader fighting a battle for all of us. She was carrying the flag." It was fitting that Billie Jean was named one of *Life* magazine's one hundred most influential people of the twentieth century.

WOMEN'S PAY IS FROM VENUS

Venus (*left*) and Serena Williams are beneficiaries of the work done by Billie Jean King.

One player who was deeply influenced by Billie Jean King was Venus Williams. Both Venus and Billie Jean learned on public courts in Southern California. Both players were outsiders, set apart from the tennis establishment—Billie Jean for her working-class roots and Venus for her African-American heritage. Both took the tennis world to task for unequal pay for male and female players.

In 2006, Wimbledon still did not offer equal prize money for men and women. Fed up, Venus—who had won the Wimbledon singles title the previous year—spoke out. In an op-ed published in the *London Times*, Venus wrote, "Wimbledon has sent me a message: I'm only a second-class champion." She continued, "The decision of the All England Lawn Tennis Club yet again to treat women as lesser players than men—undeserving of the same amount of prize money—has a particular sting."

She made several cogent points about the problems with Wimbledon's stance. She then pointed out that the All England Club had raked in profits of £25 million the previous year. "So the refusal of the All England Club ... to pay equal prize money can't be about cash. It can only be trying to make a social and political point, one that is out of step with modern society." Venus vowed to "keep doing everything I can until Billie Jean's original dream of equality is made real."

Venus prevailed. In 2007, for the first time ever, Wimbledon offered equal prize money for men and women, and fittingly, it was Venus who brought home the biggest check. For winning the Wimbledon singles title for the fourth time, Venus earned $1.4 million—the same amount as the men's singles champion, Roger Federer.

"No one loves tennis more than Billie Jean King," Venus said from Centre Court after her win. She looked up at Billie Jean, who was in the stands. "I love you," Venus said. "I wouldn't be here without you." Billie Jean waved to Venus, and Venus waved back.

Billie Jean wanted more than equal pay for female tennis players. She wanted equal opportunities for girls in all types of sports. It particularly bothered her that there were no athletic scholarships for girls at colleges and universities. She'd felt that sting personally when she was a student at Los Angeles State University. "Even though I was the best player on campus and one of the best female players in the world and easily the best-known athlete at the college, I didn't get a nickel's worth of assistance," she said.

All that changed with the passage of Title IX of the Education Amendments Act in 1972. It stated, "No person in the United States shall, on the basis of sex, be excluded from participation in, be denied the benefits of, or be subjected to discrimination under any educational program or activity receiving Federal financial assistance." Because athletics are considered an "educational program or activity," they were covered. In other words, according to the WSF, "Title IX gives women athletes the right to equal opportunity in sports in educational institutions that receive federal funds, from elementary schools to colleges and universities," noting that "almost all colleges and universities, private and public, receive such funding."

Title IX is, in the words of the WSF, "an important civil rights act that guarantees that our daughters and sons are treated in a like manner with regard to all educational programs and activities, including sports." Billie Jean wholeheartedly agreed, calling it "the third most important piece of legislation in the twentieth century. There was the vote, civil rights in the '60s, and Title IX in the '70s."

Title IX has proven remarkably effective. According to the National Coalition for Women and Girls in Education, fewer than 295,000 girls participated in high school varsity athletics in 1971, comprising just 7 percent of all varsity athletes. By 2001, "that number leaped to 2.8 million, or 41.5 percent of all varsity athletes." Colleges and universities saw similar results. In 1966, just 16,000 females competed in intercollegiate athletics, but by 2001, "that number jumped to more than 150,000"—or 43 percent of all college athletes.

Title IX provided the legal structure for opportunity for women and girls, but King was the catalyst for change. After the King-Riggs match, women got off the sidelines and began running, joining gyms, and picking up rackets. Corporations began providing sponsorships for women's events.

In talking about the match, King told *Newsweek* magazine, "I just had to play … Title IX had just passed, and I … wanted to change the hearts and minds of people to match the legislation."

King never wavered in her support of the legislation. In 2012, forty years after it was passed, she testified on behalf of Title IX before the US Senate and served on a Title IX panel at the White House.

Later in life, Billie Jean's activism on behalf of the LGBT community added to her legacy. Although slow to accept her own sexuality, Billie Jean now works tirelessly to promote equality for all people, including members of the LGBT

Billie Jean King speaks at the White House at an event honoring the thirty-seventh anniversary of the enactment of Title IX. Next to King are Education Secretary Arne Duncan and White House Senior Advisor Valerie Jarrett.

community. "The amount of untapped human potential in our world is enormous, yet in so many places, challenges like gender, race, and sexuality are used to discriminate against women and men and prevent them from reaching their full potential," King said, according to the *Huffington Post*. "We need leaders, in both the public and private sectors, to look at differences in the workplace through a lens where individuals are embraced for their unique contributions rather than judged, discounted, or alienated for what makes them different." To achieve this, Billie Jean launched the Billie Jean King Leadership Initiative in 2014. Its mission, in the organization's own words, is to "move the needle on issues impacting diverse talent globally."

Billie Jean takes the notion of legacy seriously. "I see leaving a legacy as building a wall," she said. "We left the wall one brick higher than the people before us, and the next generation is going to set another brick and make it even higher."

Outstanding Honors

It's no surprise that King has received countless awards and honors over the years, both on and off the court. Three in particular stand out.

The Arthur Ashe Courage Award

One is the Arthur Ashe Courage Award, which she received in 1999. This award is part of the larger ESPY Awards program. (The ESPY Award, short for Excellence in Sports Performance Yearly Award, is given by ESPN to recognize achievement in sports—similar to the Grammys for music, the Emmys for TV, the Tonys for theater, and the Oscars for film.) The Arthur Ashe Courage Award is named after tennis player Arthur Ashe. A contemporary and close friend of Billie Jean's, Ashe took the tennis world by storm, becoming the only black man to win the singles title at Wimbledon, at the US Open, and at the Australian Open. He twice held the world number one position, in 1968 and 1975, before retiring in 1980. He formed the Association of Tennis Professionals (ATP) and fought racism, even challenging apartheid in South Africa. Ashe's life was cut tragically short after he contracted HIV from a blood transfusion he received during heart bypass surgery. Before his death in 1993, Ashe worked tirelessly to educate others about HIV and AIDS, founding the Arthur Ashe Foundation for the Defeat of AIDS and the Arthur Ashe Institute for Urban Health. The award, typically (although not always) given to individuals in the world of athletics, recognizes those whose contributions "transcend sports." Apart from King, other recipients have included Howard Cosell (who, coincidentally, served as the television commentator during the Battle of the Sexes), Muhammad Ali, Pat Tillman, Nelson Mandela, and more recently, Caitlyn Jenner.

Renaming of the National Tennis Center

In addition to winning the Arthur Ashe Courage Award, Billie Jean was honored by the United States Tennis Association (formerly the United States Lawn Tennis Association). It renamed the USTA National Tennis Center the USTA Billie Jean King National Tennis Center. This was to recognize Billie Jean's contributions to tennis, sports, and society as a whole. The facility in Queens, New York, is where the US Open is played each year. It features twelve indoor courts, nineteen outdoor courts, and three stadium courts, including the famed Arthur Ashe Stadium. The USTA Billie Jean King National Tennis Center is not just for the pros, however. The facility is open to the public for recreational play—much like the public courts in Long Beach, where Billie Jean learned to play.

Jimmy Connors, John McEnroe, Chris Evert, and Venus Williams (*back row from left*) honored Billie Jean King at the ceremony commemorating the renaming of the US Open venue on August 28, 2006.

The center was renamed on August 28, 2006, and marked with a special ceremony held in Billie Jean's honor. In attendance were fellow tennis greats Chris Evert, Venus Williams, John McEnroe, and Jimmy Connors, who all spoke at the affair. In his remarks, McEnroe called Billie Jean "the single most important person in the history of women's sports." Perhaps more importantly, the notoriously brash McEnroe admitted that Billie Jean changed his own views on female athletes. Recalling the Battle of the Sexes, McEnroe said, "I was a fourteen-year-old male chauvinist pig when they played, hoping Riggs would kick Billie

Jean's ---. But now, as the father of four girls, I want to say for the record that I'm very happy Billie Jean won!"

The Presidential Medal of Freedom

No doubt the Arthur Ashe Courage Award and the renaming of the USTA National Tennis Center were very meaningful to King, but on August 12, 2009, she received the honor of a lifetime. On that day, in the White House, President Barack Obama presented her with the highest civilian award in the United States: the Presidential Medal of Freedom. This medal recognizes people who have made "an especially meritorious contribution to the security or national interests of the United States, world peace, cultural or other significant public or private endeavors."

King was the first female athlete ever to win the award. When she received the medal from the president, Billie Jean—accompanied by her long-time partner Ilana Kloss and her mother Betty (her father Bill had passed away in 2006)—kissed it.

In describing that year's field of Presidential Medal of Freedom recipients—which also included such luminaries as Professor Steven Hawking, Senator Edward Kennedy, Supreme Court Justice Sandra Day O'Connor, actor Sidney Poitier, actress Chita Rivera, and South African anti-apartheid activist Desmond Tutu—President Obama noted, "They each share one overarching trait: each has been an agent of change. Each saw an imperfect world and set about improving it, often overcoming great obstacles along the way."

For her part, Billie Jean was recognized for her ongoing fight for equality. "We honor what she calls 'all the off-the-court stuff,'" said Obama. He explained, "What she did to broaden the reach of the game, to change how women athletes and women everywhere view themselves, and to give everyone, regardless of gender or sexual orientation—including my two daughters—a chance to compete both on the court and in life."

GLOSSARY

career Grand Slam The act of winning all four Grand Slam tournaments over the course of a player's career.

doubles A tennis match in which a team of two athletes plays against another team of two athletes.

drop shot A shot in which the ball is struck softly, landing just over the net.

finals The round in a tournament in which two players or teams remain. Whoever wins the final round wins the tournament.

game A component of a tennis set in which a minimum of four points must be won. To win a set, a player must win at least six games.

genteel A term meaning polite, refined, or respectable; usually describes the behaviors of upper-class society.

Grand Slam The act of winning all four Grand Slam tournaments in a single calendar year.

Grand Slam tournament One of four prestigious tennis tournaments: the Australian Open, the French Open, the US Open, and Wimbledon.

lob A shot hit high in the air with the purpose of landing behind the opponent or to give a person time to get back into position after chasing a good shot.

match A tennis contest consisting of best-of-three or best-of-five sets.

mixed doubles A tennis match in which a team of two athletes plays against another team of two athletes. In mixed doubles, each team is composed of a man and a woman.

Open Era An era in tennis in which professionals and amateurs were permitted to play in Grand Slam and other prestigious tournaments in which prize money was awarded. The Open Era began in 1968.

quarterfinals The round in a tournament in which eight players or teams remain.

racket From the Arabic *rakhat*, meaning "palm of the hand," a type of bat with a round or oval frame and strings in the middle.

semifinals The round in a tournament in which four players or teams remain.

serve The shot that puts the point into play.

set A component of a tennis match. To win a match, a player must win a prescribed number of sets. In major tournaments, men must win three out of five and women two out of three.

singles A match in which one athlete plays against another.

unseeded A person or a team not ranked among those expected to win a tennis tournament. The best entrant in the tournament is the top seed.

Wimbledon triple The act of winning the Wimbledon singles, doubles, and mixed doubles titles in a single year.

SELECTED BIBLIOGRAPHY

Books

King, Billie Jean, and Frank Deford. *Billie Jean.* New York: Viking Press, 1982.

King, Billie Jean. *Pressure Is a Privilege: Lessons I've Learned from Life and the Battle of the Sexes.* New York: LifeTime Media Inc., 2008.

Lannin, Joanne. *Billie Jean King: Tennis Trailblazer.* Minneapolis, MN: Lerner Publications, 1999.

Ware, Susan. *Game, Set, Match: Billie Jean King and the Revolution in Women's Sports.* Chapel Hill, NC: The University of North Carolina Press, 2011.

Online Articles

Adams, Cecil. "Was the 'Battle of the Sexes' Tennis Match Between Billie Jean King and Bobby Riggs Fixed?" *The Straight Dope*, December 17, 2010. Accessed June 15, 2015. www.straightdope.com/columns/read/2972/was-the-battle-of-the-sexes-tennis-match-between-billie-jean-king-and-bobby-riggs-fixed.

Brandon, Katherine. "Presidential Medal of Freedom Recipients." *The White House Blog*, July 30, 2009. Accessed June 15, 2015. www.whitehouse.gov/blog/2009-Medal-of-Freedom-Recipients.

Buzinski, Jim. "Moment #3: Tennis Great Billie Jean King Outed." *SB Nation*, October 2, 2011. Accessed June 15, 2015. www.outsports.com/2011/10/2/4051938/moment-3-tennis-great-billie-jean-king-outed.

Chapin, Kim. "Center Court Is Her Domain." *Sports Illustrated*, June 24, 1968. Accessed June 15, 2015. www.si.com/vault/1968/06/24/609164/center-court-is-her-domain.

Higdon, Hal. "Plays Tennis Like a Man, Speaks Out Like—Billie Jean King." *New York Times*, August 27, 1967. Accessed June 25, 2015. www.nytimes.com/2013/08/25/magazine/plays-tennis-like-a-man-speaks-out- like-billie-jean-king.html?_r=0).

Khurshudyan, Isabelle. "Billie Jean King Hopes World Team Tennis Can Expand." *Washington Post*, July 11, 2014. Accessed June 15, 2015. www.washingtonpost.com/sports/othersports/billie-jean-king-hopes-world-team-tennis-can-expand/2014/07/11/d963b71a-090c-11e4-bbf1-cc51275e7f8f_story.html.

Roberts, Selena. "Tennis's Other Battle of the Sexes, Before King-Riggs." *New York Times*, August 21, 2005. www.nytimes.com/2005/08/21/sports/tennis/tenniss-other-battle-of-the-sexes-before-kingriggs.html?_r=0.

Sokol, Lori. "Billie Jean King – Rallying for a New Equality." *Huffington Post*, January 15, 2015. www.

huffingtonpost.com/lori-sokol/billie-jean-king-rallying_b_6474514.html.

Stanley, Alessandra. "The Legacy of Billie Jean King, an Athlete Who Demanded Equal Play." *New York Times*, April 26, 2006. Accessed June 15, 2015. www.nytimes.com/2006/04/26/arts/television/26stan.html?_r=0.

Van Natta Jr., Don. "The Match Maker: Bobby Riggs, The Mafia and The Battle of the Sexes." *ESPN*, August 25, 2013. espn.go.com/espn/feature/story/_/id/9589625/the-match-maker.

Williams, Venus. "Wimbledon Has Sent Me a Message: I'm Only a Second-Class Champion." *London Times*, June 26, 2006. Accessed June 15, 2015. www.thetimes.co.uk/tto/sport/tennis/article2369985.ece.

FURTHER INFORMATION

Books

King, Billie Jean, and Cynthia Starr. *We Have Come a Long Way: The Story of Women's Tennis.* New York: McGraw Hill, 1988.

Roberts, Selena. *A Necessary Spectacle: Billie Jean King, Bobby Riggs, and the Tennis Match That Leveled the Game.* New York: Crown, 2005.

Ware, Susan. *Title IX: A Brief History With Documents.* Long Grove, IL: Waveland Press, 2014.

Videos

Billie Jean King
video.pbs.org/video/2365075155
This PBS documentary profiles the life and contributions to society of Billie Jean King.

Billie Jean King on World Team Tennis Beginnings
www.youtube.com/watch?v=Hi1W_7XkRpM
The Associated Press interviews Billie Jean King about World Team Tennis and why she founded the competitive league for men and women.

Significance of Title IX
www.youtube.com/watch?v=C4klR1FVbaI
Billie Jean King discusses the significance of this landmark

legislation, which brought athletic opportunity for girls and women in our schools and colleges, with ESPN.

"This Week" Sunday Spotlight: Billie Jean King
www.youtube.com/watch?v=MyMtOwwtJW0
Billie Jean reflects on the Battle of the Sexes forty years later.

Organizations

Billie Jean King Leadership Initiative
www.bjkli.org

International Tennis Hall of Fame
www.tennisfame.com

Women's Sports Foundation
www.womenssportsfoundation.org

Women's Tennis Association
www.wtatennis.com

INDEX

ABOUT THE AUTHOR

Kate Shoup has written more than thirty books and has edited hundreds more. When not working, Kate loves to watch IndyCar racing, ski, read, and ride her motorcycle. She lives in Indianapolis, Indiana, with her husband, her daughter, and their dog. To learn more about Kate and her work, visit www.kateshoup.com.

DA   12/16 ✓